The Adventures of Scuba Jack
Copyright 2021 by Beth Costanzo
All rights reserved

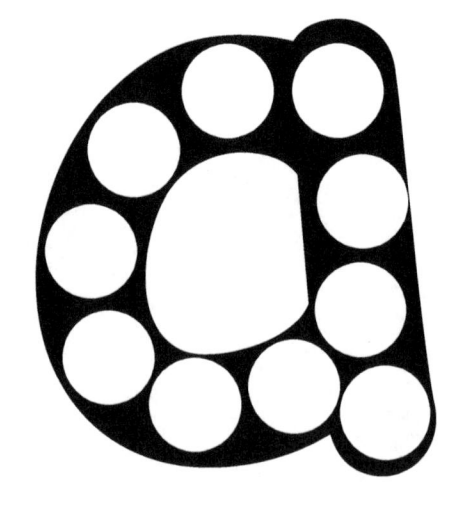

a is for alligator

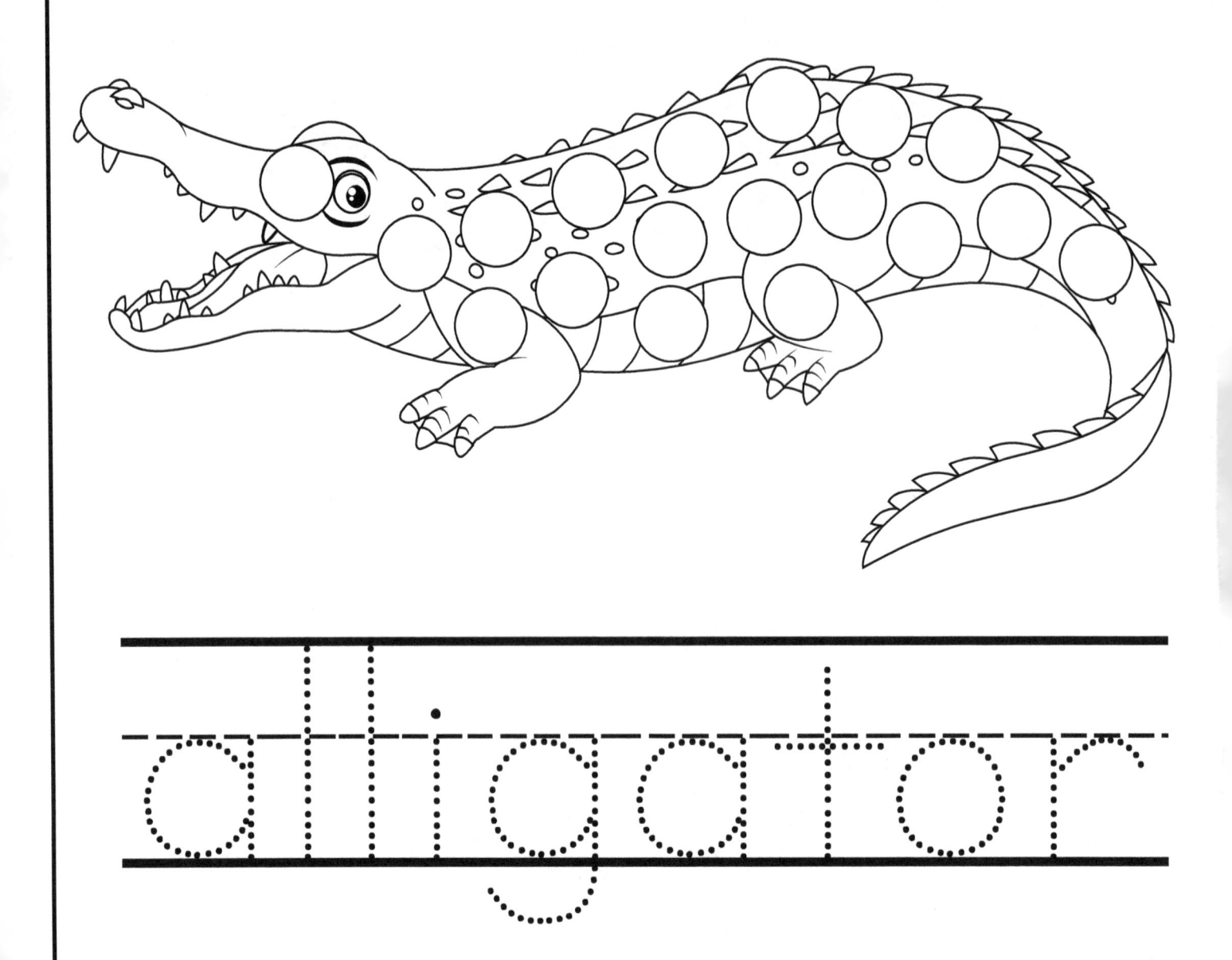

alligator

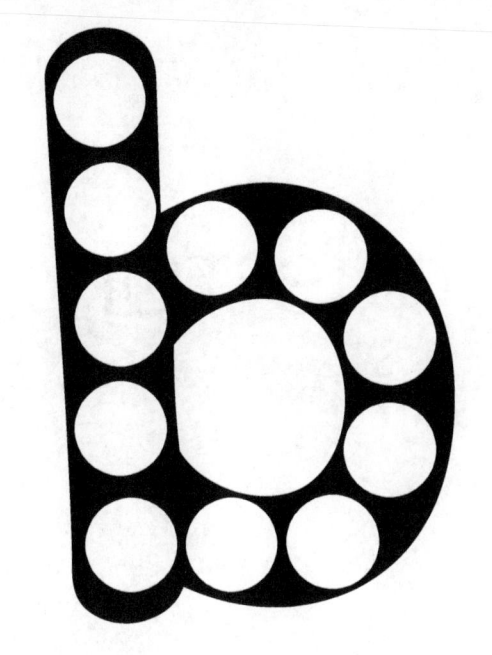

b is for bear

bear

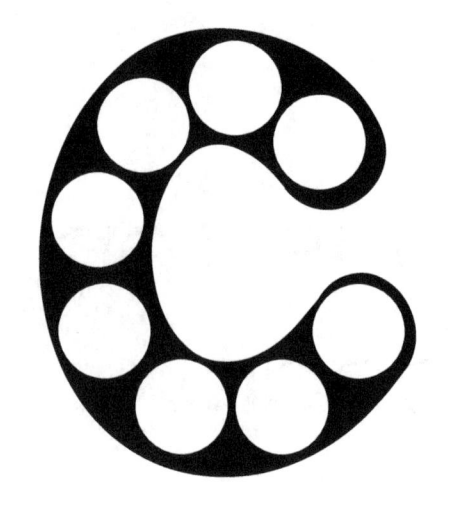

c is for cat

cat

d is for dinosaur

dinosaur

e is for elephant

elephant

f is for fish

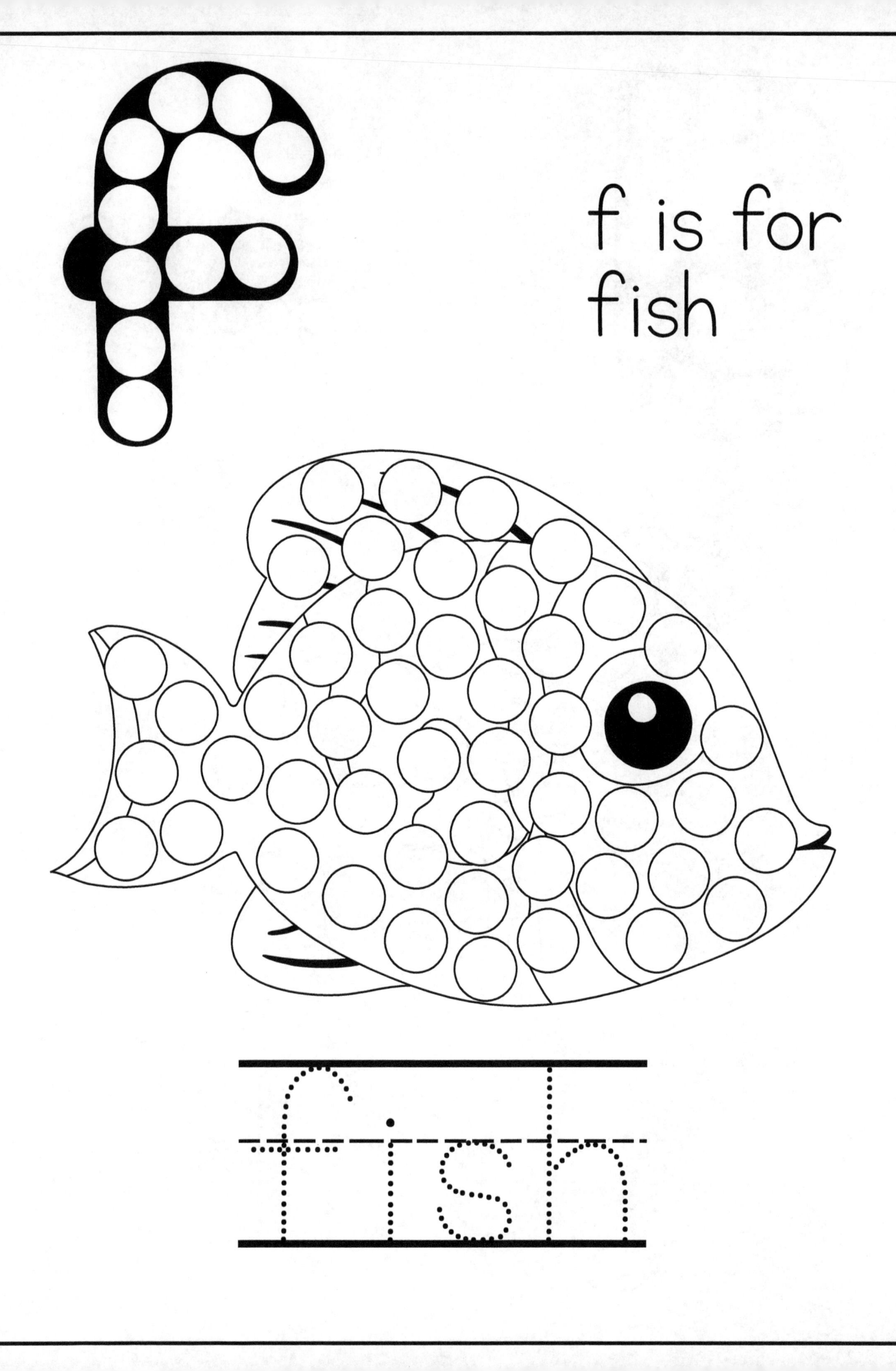

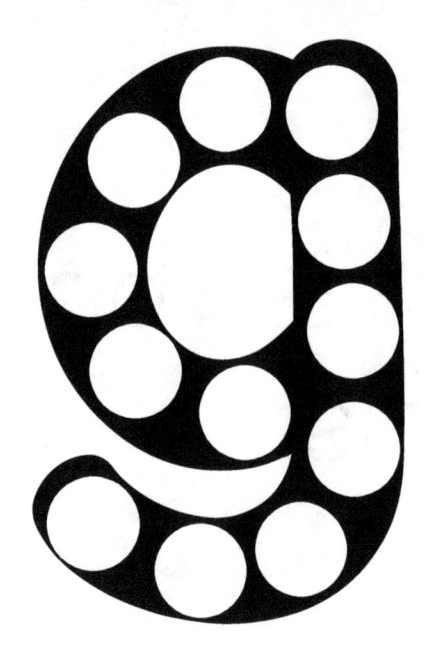

g is for goat

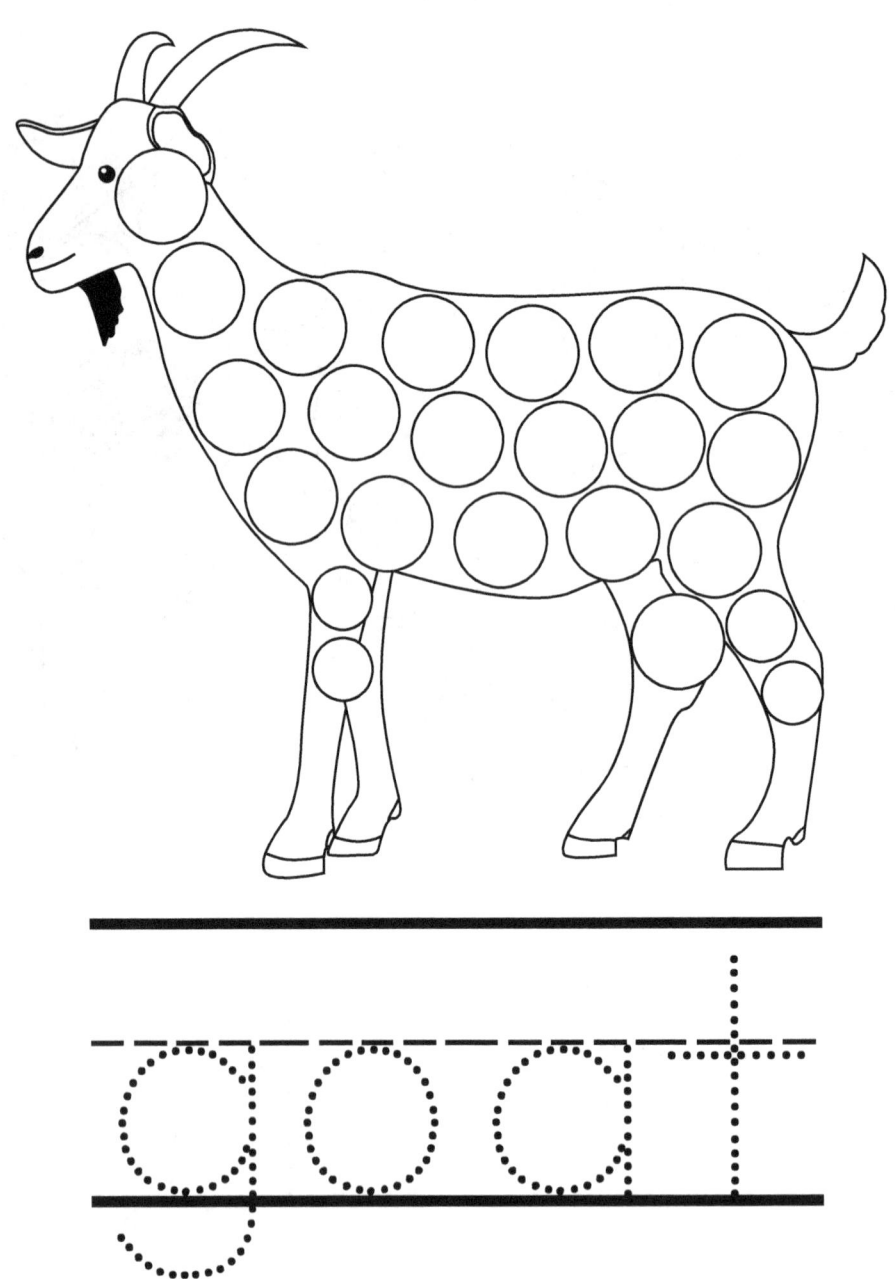

goat

h is for horse

horse

i is for iguana

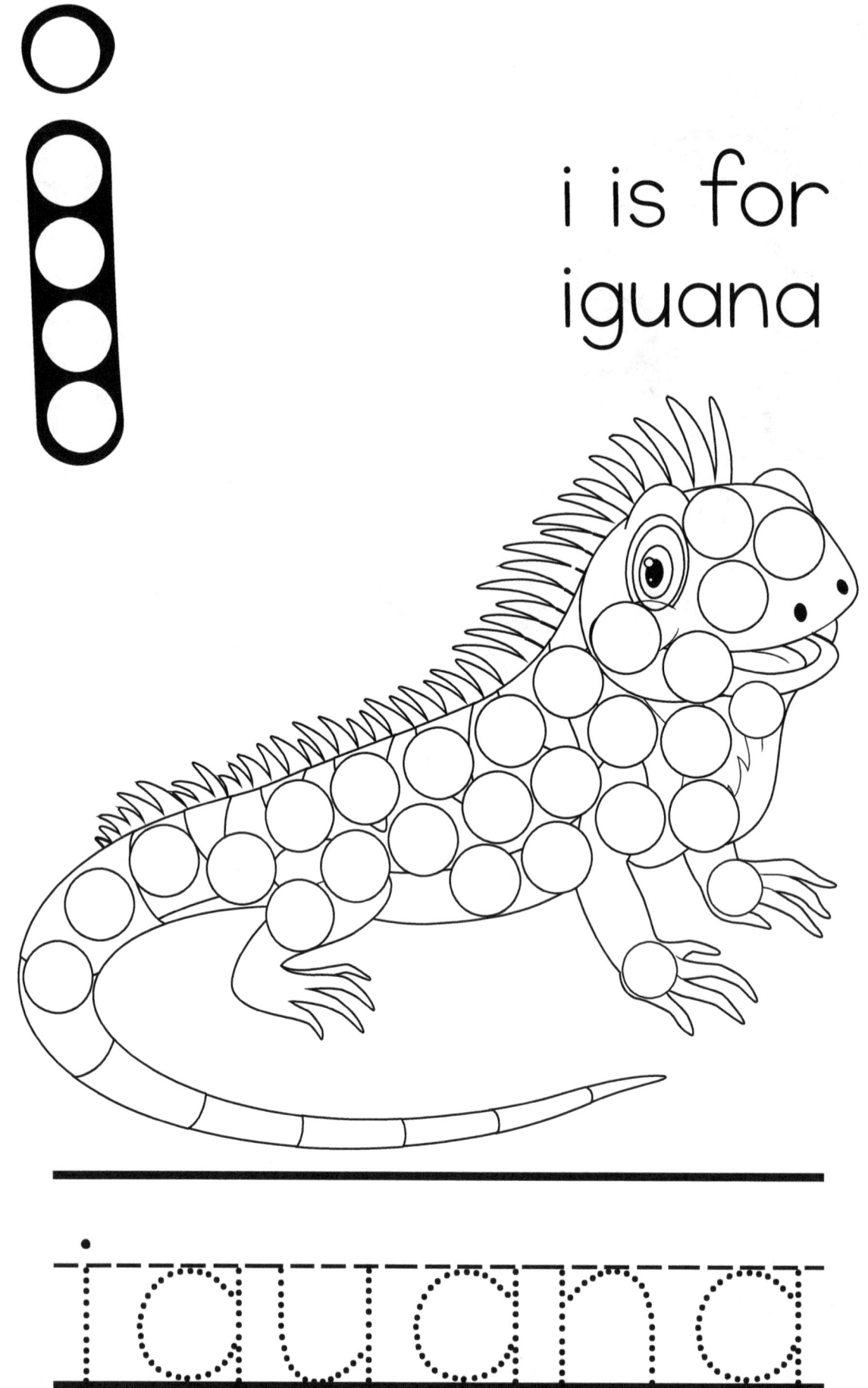

iguana

j is for jellyfish

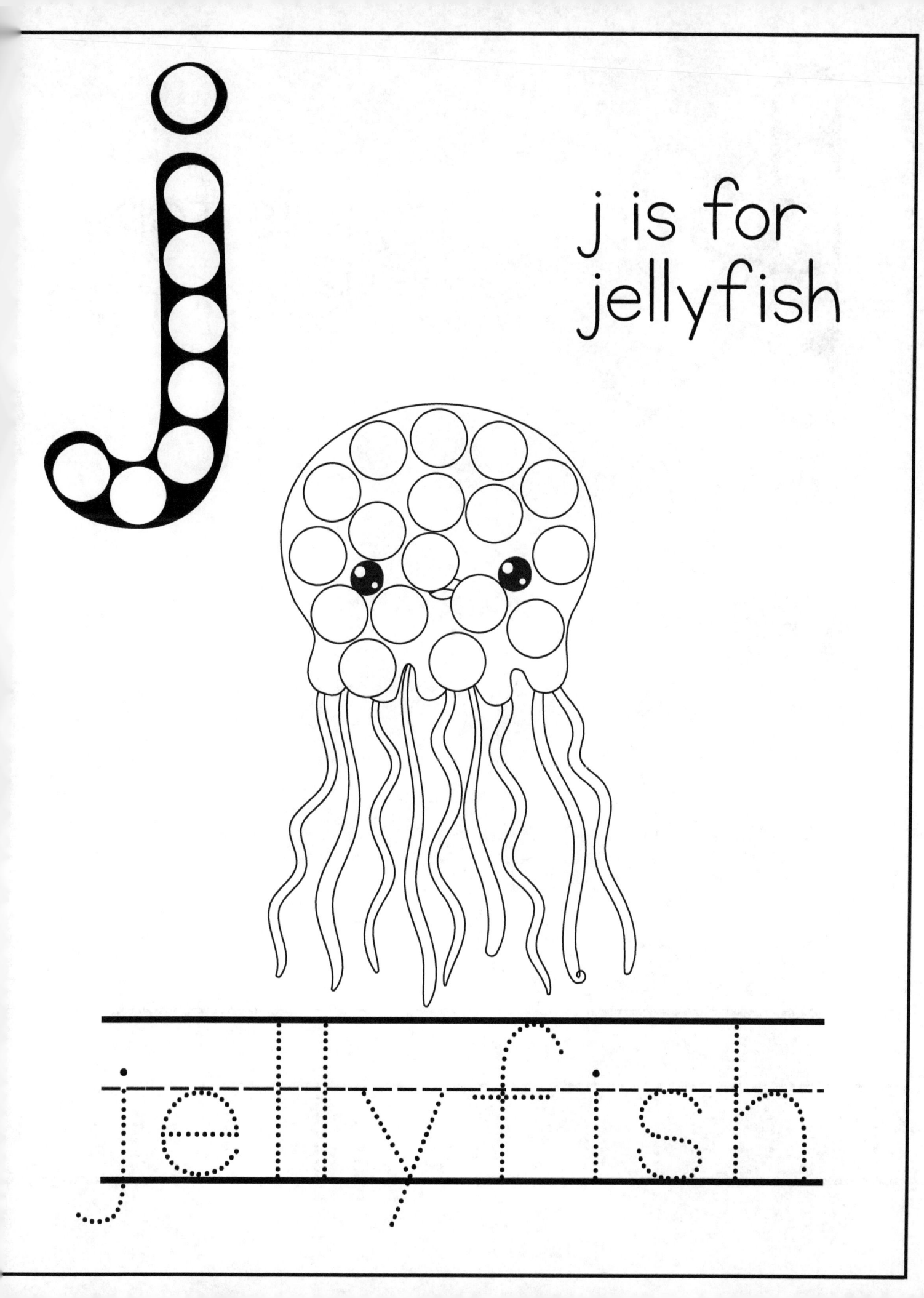

jellyfish

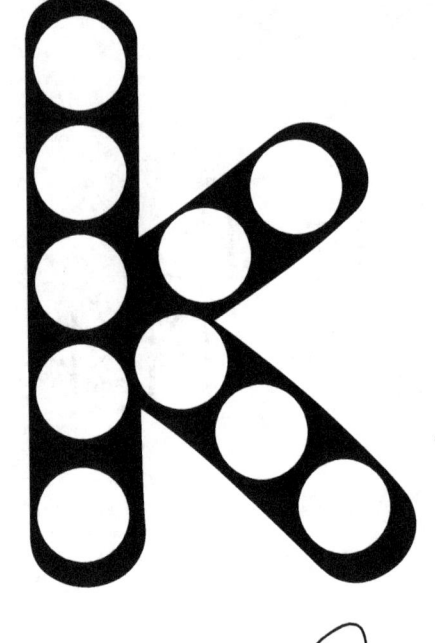

k is for kangaroo

kangaroo

l is for lion

lion

m is for monkey

monkey

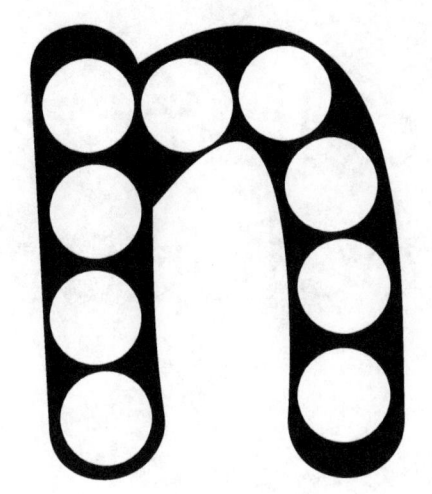

n is for
narwhal

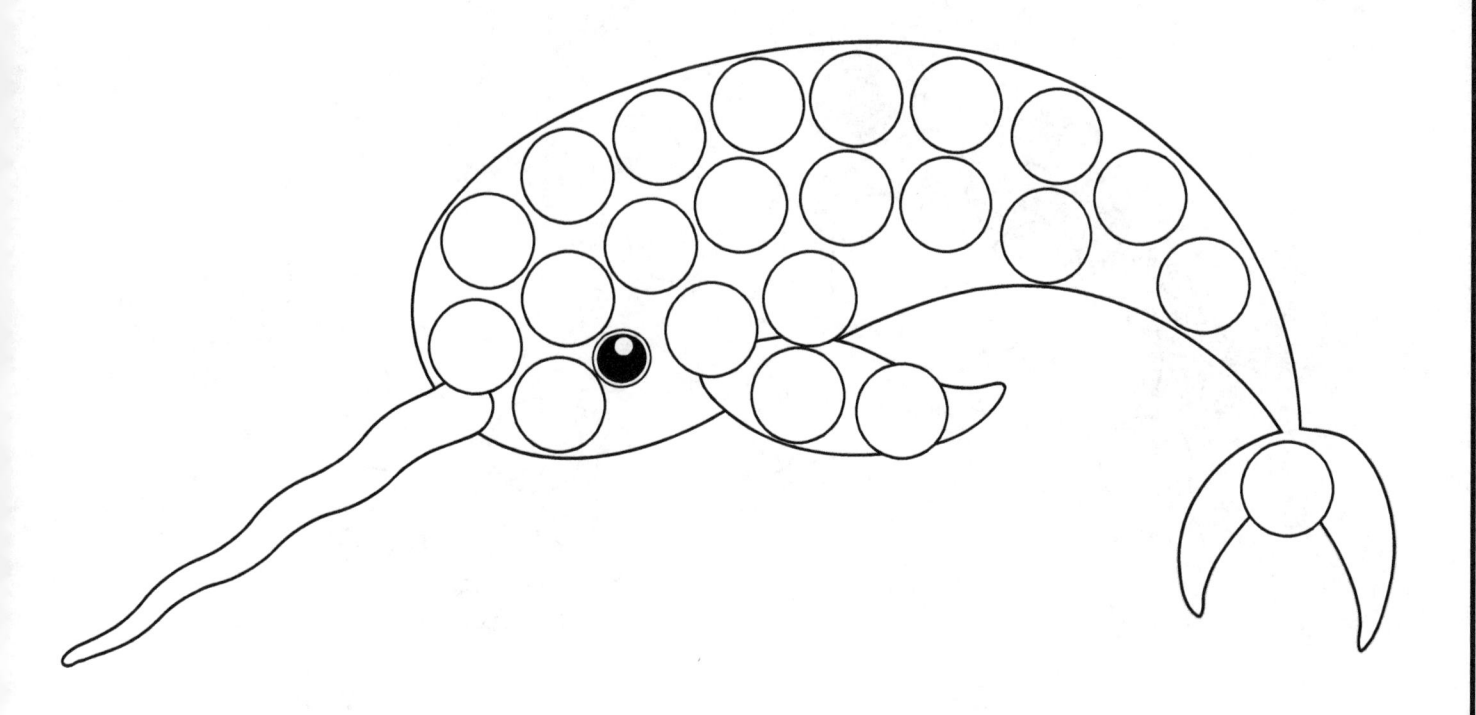

narwhal

o is for
octopus

octopus

p is for penguin

penguin

q is for quail

quail

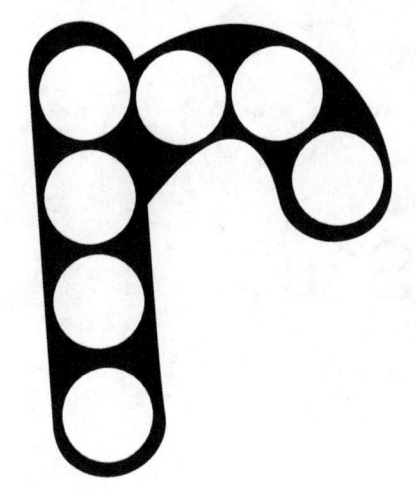

r is for rhinoceros

rhinoceros

s is for seal

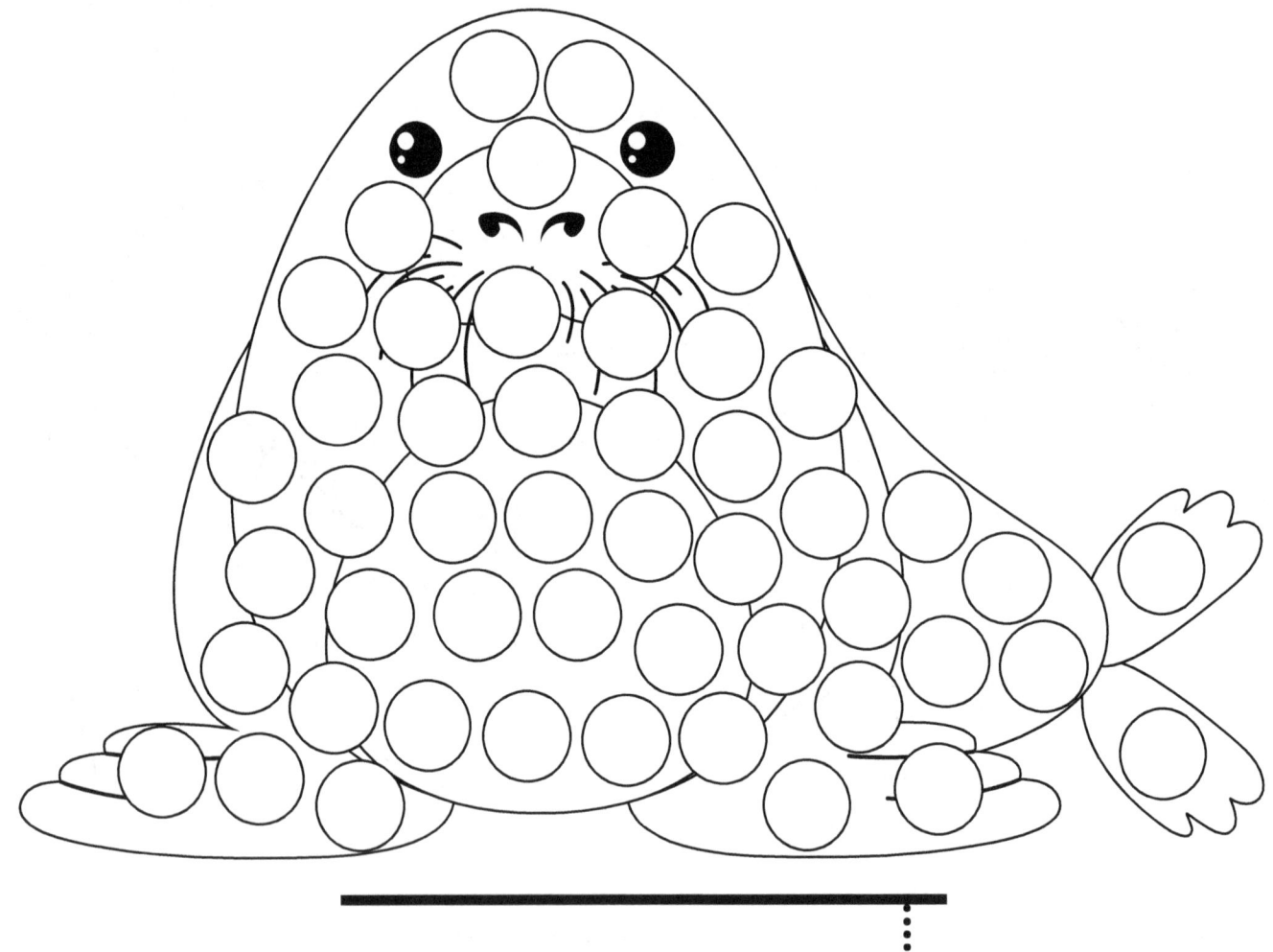

seal

t is for tiger

tiger

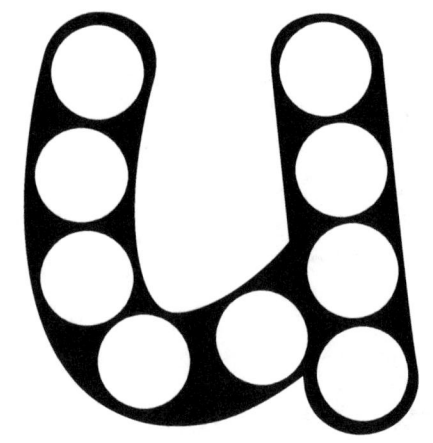

u is for urchin

urchin

v is for vulture

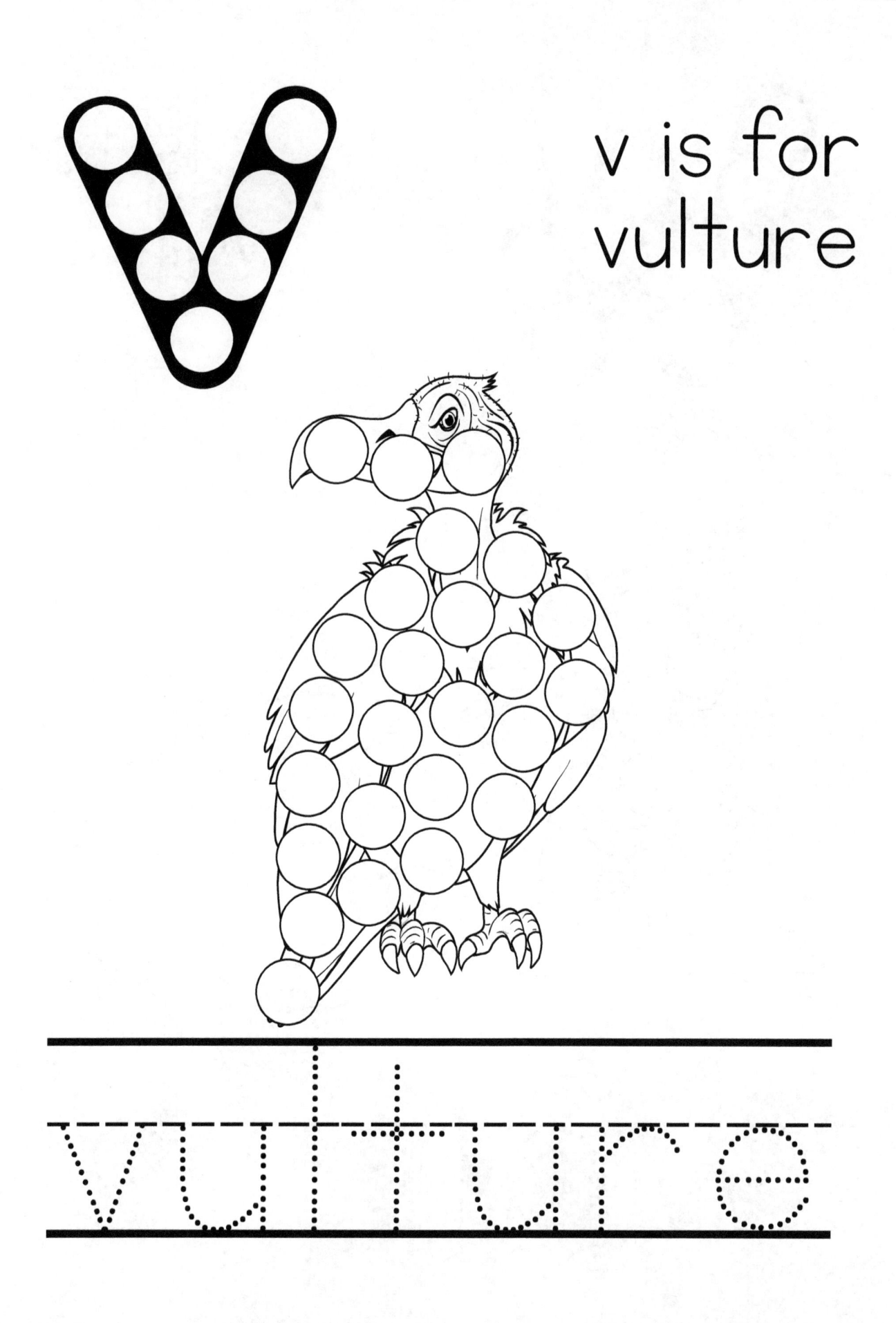

vulture

w is for walrus

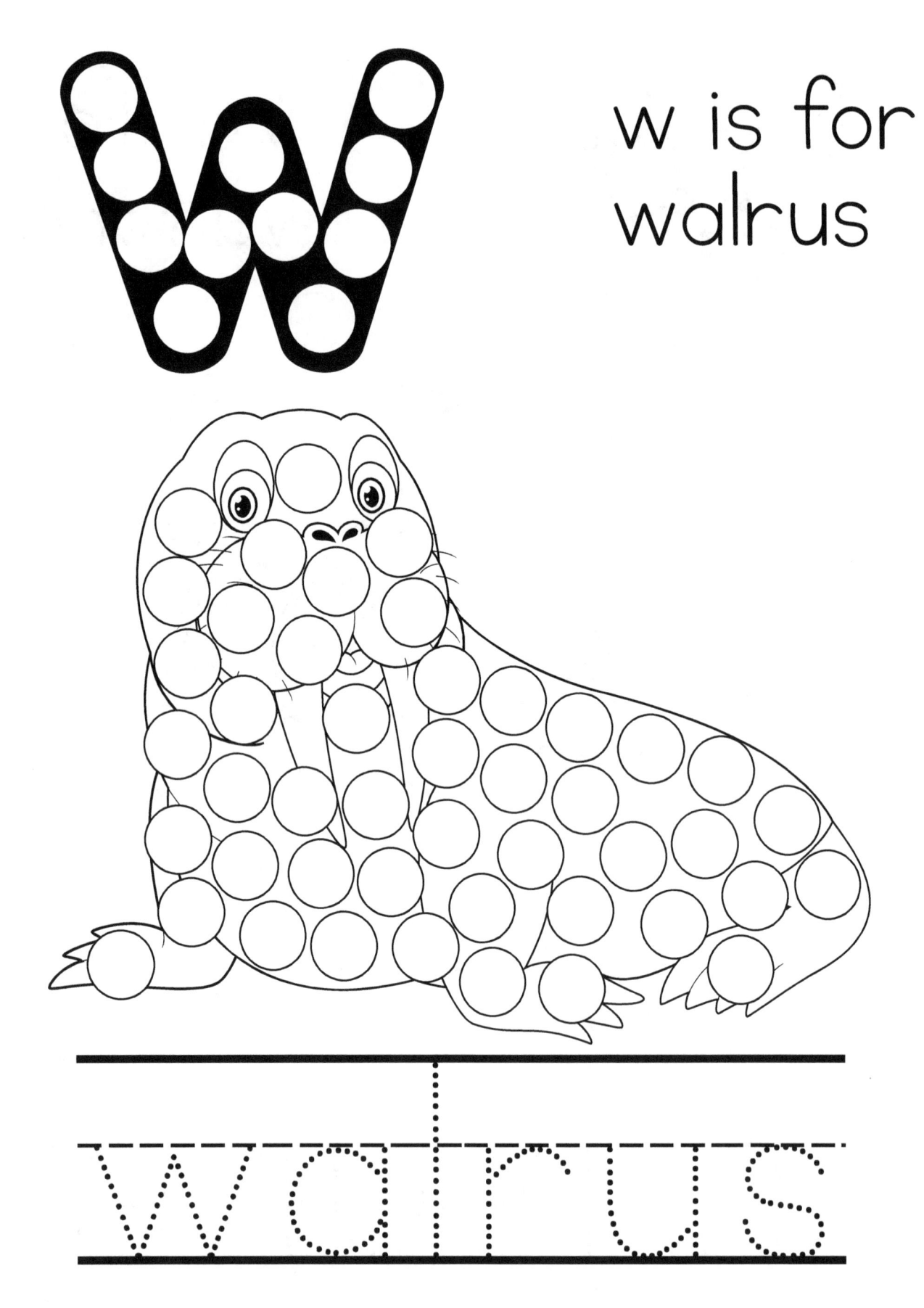

walrus

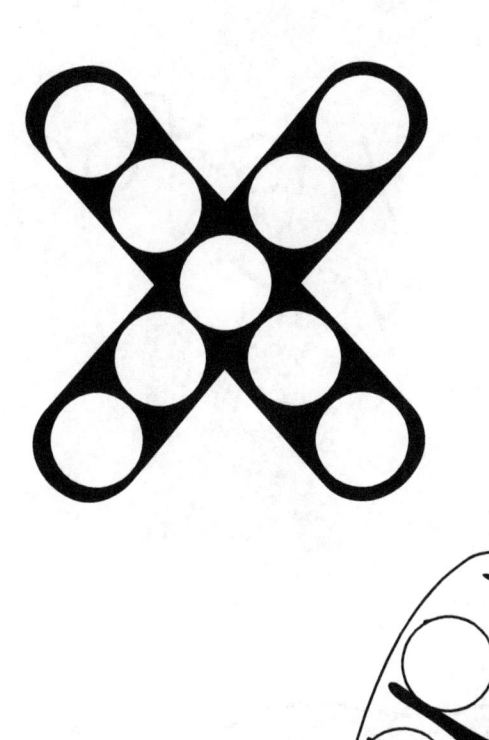

x is for
x-ray fish

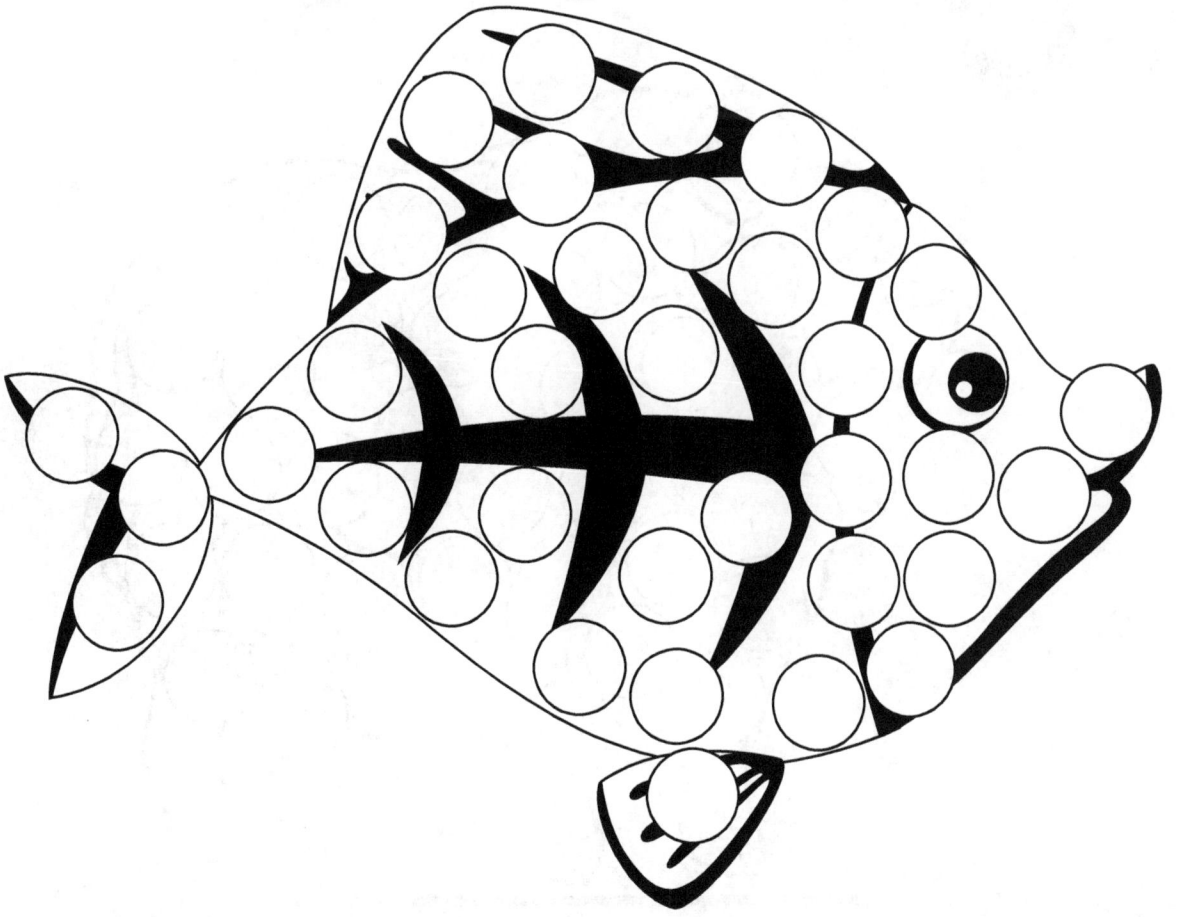

x-ray fish

y is for yak

yak

z is for zebra

zebra

Visit us at:
www.adventuresofscubajack.com

CPSIA information can be obtained
at www.ICGtesting.com
Printed in the USA
LVHW020952020623
748732LV00013B/124

9 781087 957876